T0400242

THE PITTSBURGH STEELERS

BY ALICIA Z. KLEPEIS

EPIC

BELLWETHER MEDIA ★ MINNEAPOLIS, MN

EPIC

EPIC BOOKS are no ordinary books. They burst with intense action, high-speed heroics, and shadows of the unknown. Are you ready for an Epic adventure?

This edition first published in 2024 by Bellwether Media, Inc.

Library of Congress Cataloging-in-Publication Data

Names: Klepeis, Alicia, 1971- author.
Title: The Pittsburgh Steelers / by Alicia Z. Klepeis.
Description: Minneapolis, MN : Bellwether Media, 2024. | Series: Epic. NFL team profiles | Includes bibliographical references and index. | Audience: Ages 7-12 | Audience: Grades 2-3 | Summary: "Engaging images accompany information about the Pittsburgh Steelers. The combination of high-interest subject matter and light text is intended for students in grades 2 through 7"-- Provided by publisher.
Identifiers: LCCN 2023021960 (print) | LCCN 2023021961 (ebook) | ISBN 9798886874921 (library binding) | ISBN 9798886876802 (ebook)
Subjects: LCSH: Pittsburgh Steelers (Football team)--History--Juvenile literature.
Classification: LCC GV956.P57 K (print) | LCC GV956.P57 (ebook) | DDC 796.332/640974886--dc23/eng/20230515
LC record available at https://lccn.loc.gov/2023021960
LC ebook record available at https://lccn.loc.gov/2023021961

Editor: Kieran Downs   Designer: Josh Brink

Printed in the United States of America, North Mankato, MN.

TABLE OF CONTENTS

OUTSTANDING IN OVERTIME

NAJEE HARRIS

On January 9, 2022, the Steelers face the Ravens. The game goes into overtime.

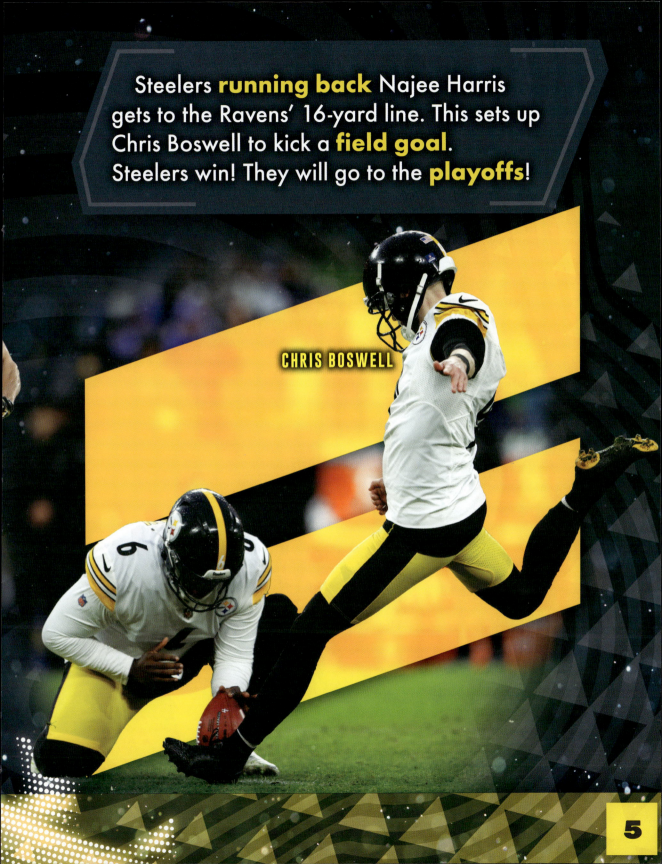

Steelers **running back** Najee Harris gets to the Ravens' 16-yard line. This sets up Chris Boswell to kick a **field goal**. Steelers win! They will go to the **playoffs**!

CHRIS BOSWELL

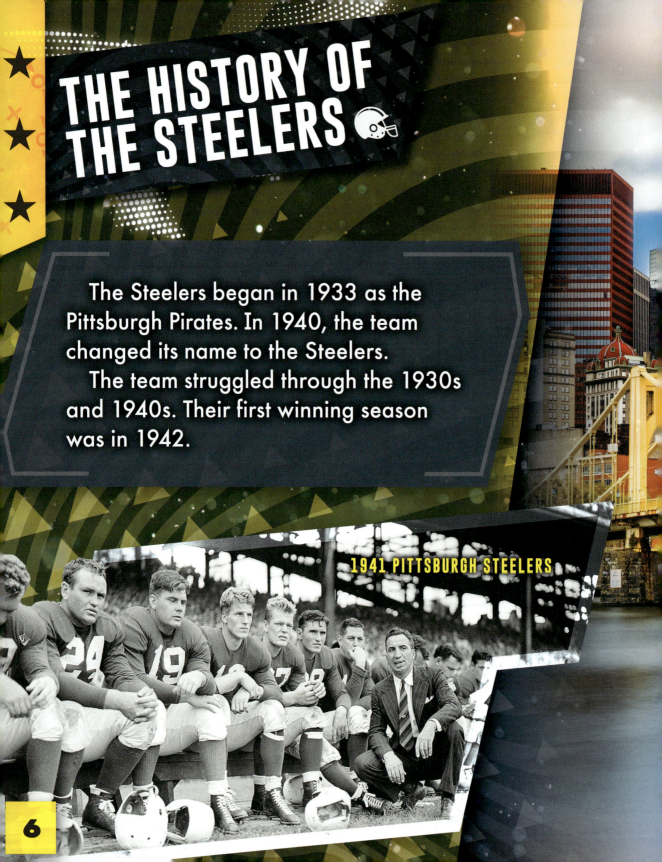

THE HISTORY OF THE STEELERS

The Steelers began in 1933 as the Pittsburgh Pirates. In 1940, the team changed its name to the Steelers.

The team struggled through the 1930s and 1940s. Their first winning season was in 1942.

1941 PITTSBURGH STEELERS

Pittsburgh, Pennsylvania, once made much of the steel in the United States. The name *Steelers* comes from the city's many steelworkers.

PITTSBURGH, PENNSYLVANIA

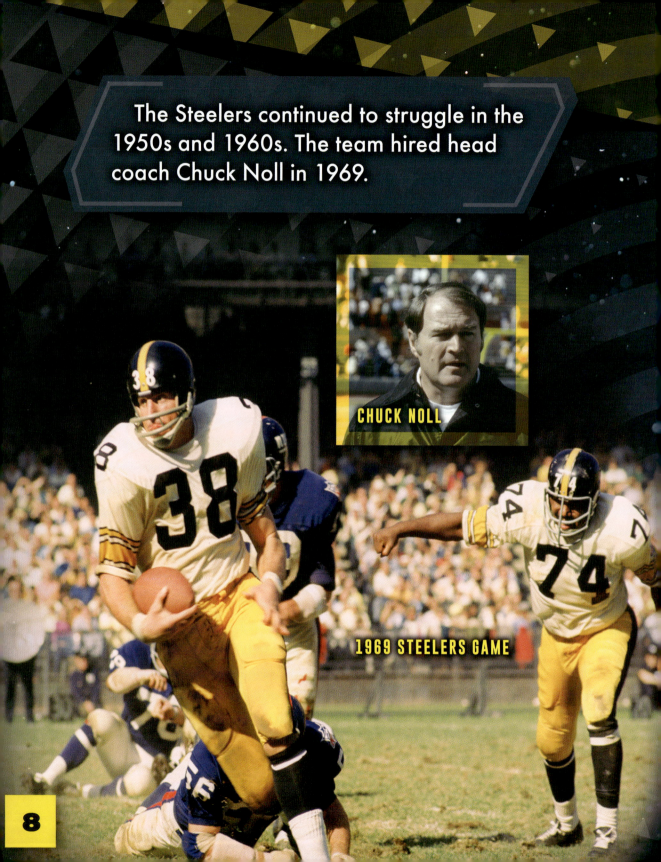

The Steelers continued to struggle in the 1950s and 1960s. The team hired head coach Chuck Noll in 1969.

CHUCK NOLL

1969 STEELERS GAME

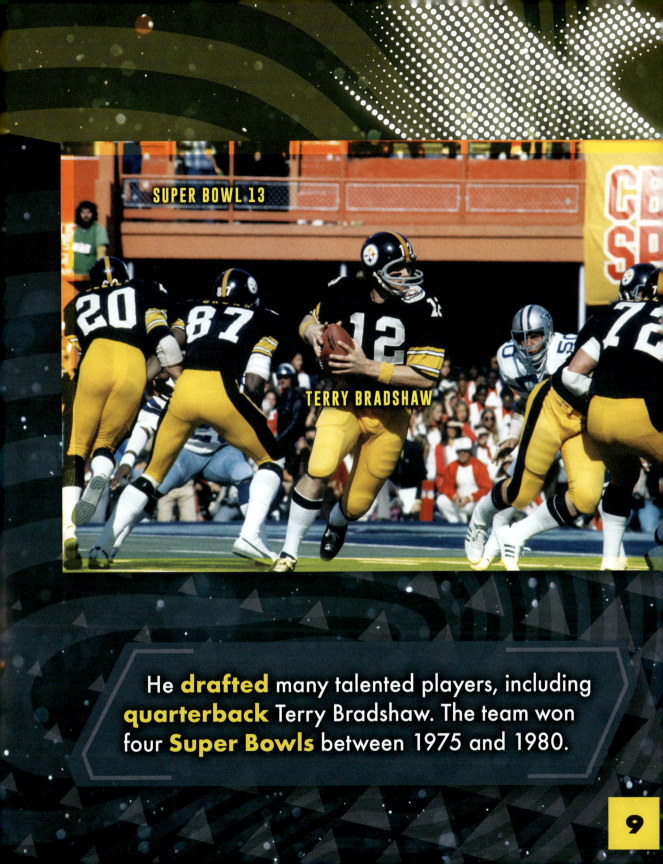

SUPER BOWL 13

TERRY BRADSHAW

He **drafted** many talented players, including **quarterback** Terry Bradshaw. The team won four **Super Bowls** between 1975 and 1980.

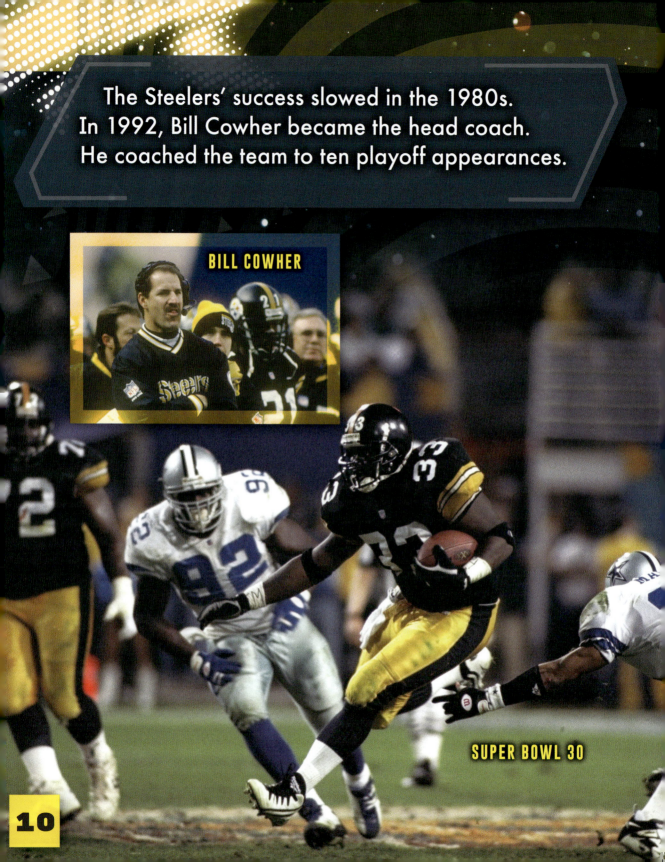

The Steelers' success slowed in the 1980s. In 1992, Bill Cowher became the head coach. He coached the team to ten playoff appearances.

BILL COWHER

SUPER BOWL 30

In 1996, the Steelers played in Super Bowl 30. But they lost to the Dallas Cowboys.

TROPHY CASE

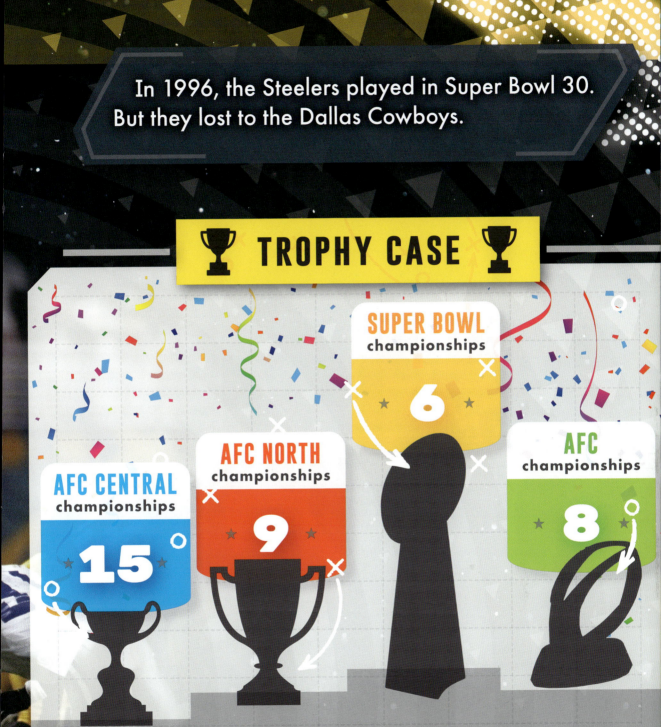

SUPER BOWL championships
6

AFC CENTRAL championships
15

AFC NORTH championships
9

AFC championships
8

The Steelers continued their strong play in the early 2000s. They won the Super Bowl in 2006 and 2009.

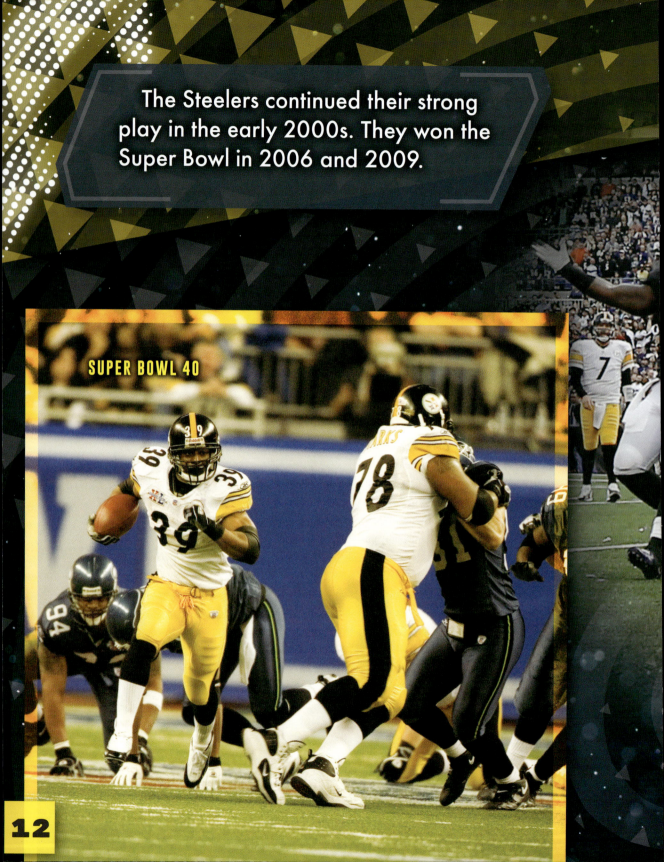

SUPER BOWL 40

The Steelers were the first team to win six Super Bowls.

2015 STEELERS GAME

The Steelers had a winning record for much of the 2010s. They returned to the playoffs six times during these years!

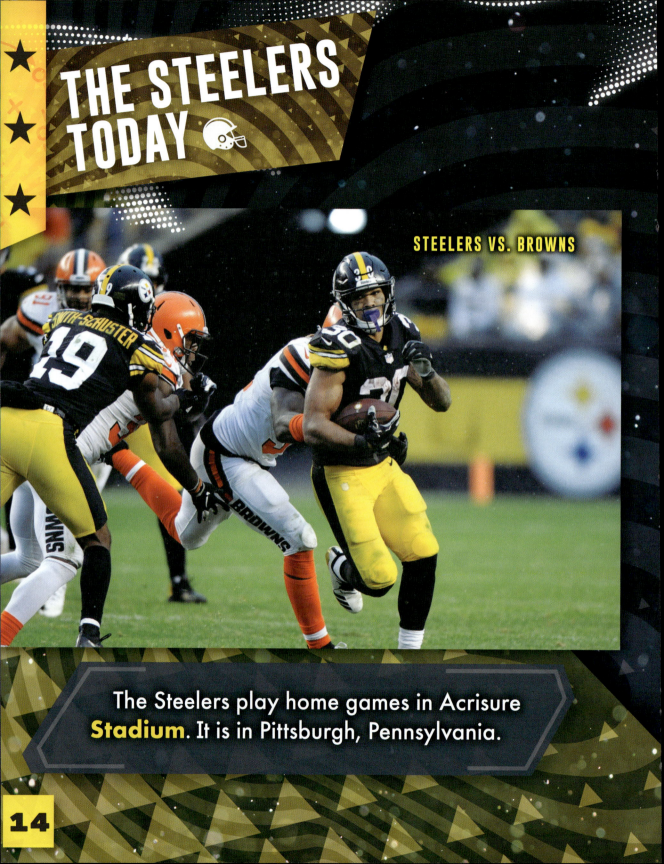

THE STEELERS TODAY

STEELERS VS. BROWNS

The Steelers play home games in Acrisure **Stadium**. It is in Pittsburgh, Pennsylvania.

The team plays in the AFC North **division**. One main **rival** is the Baltimore Ravens. Another is the Cleveland Browns.

📍 LOCATION 📍

PENNSYLVANIA

ACRISURE STADIUM
Pittsburgh, Pensylvania

N
W E
S

GAME DAY!

Steelers fans call themselves Steeler Nation. They wear black and gold. These are the team colors.

Steely McBeam is the team's **mascot**. On game day, he dances and hangs out with fans.

STEELY McBEAM

ACRISURE STADIUM

Steelers fans wave Terrible Towels to cheer on their team. The towels have been a part of game day since 1975.

The team's fight song is "Here We Go." Fans sing and cheer for their favorite team!

TRAVELING TOWELS

Steelers fans have taken Terrible Towels to many places. They have been to the South Pole, Mount Everest, and even outer space!

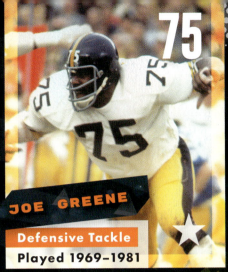

75

JOE GREENE

Defensive Tackle
Played 1969–1981

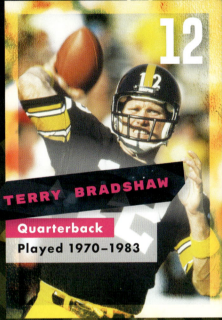

12

TERRY BRADSHAW

Quarterback
Played 1970–1983

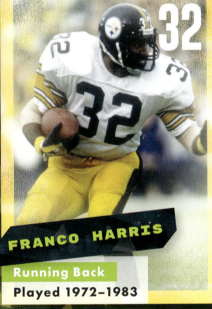

32

FRANCO HARRIS

Running Back
Played 1972–1983

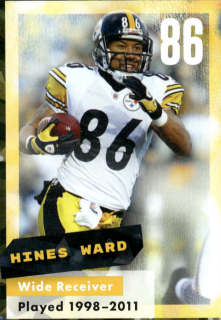

86

HINES WARD

Wide Receiver
Played 1998–2011

7

BEN ROETHLISBERGER

Quarterback
Played 2004–2021

PITTSBURGH STEELERS FACTS

LOGO

JOINED THE NFL | **1933**

NICKNAMES | The Black and Gold, Men of Steel

MASCOT

STEELY McBEAM

CONFERENCE

American Football Conference (AFC)

COLORS

DIVISION | **AFC North**

Baltimore Ravens

Cincinnati Bengals

Cleveland Browns

STADIUM

★ **ACRISURE STADIUM** ★

opened August 18, 2001

holds **68,400** people

⏱ TIMELINE

1933
The team plays its first season in the NFL

1969
Chuck Noll becomes the team's head coach

1975
The Steelers win their first Super Bowl

2009
The Steelers win their sixth Super Bowl

1980
The Steelers win their fourth Super Bowl

★ RECORDS ★

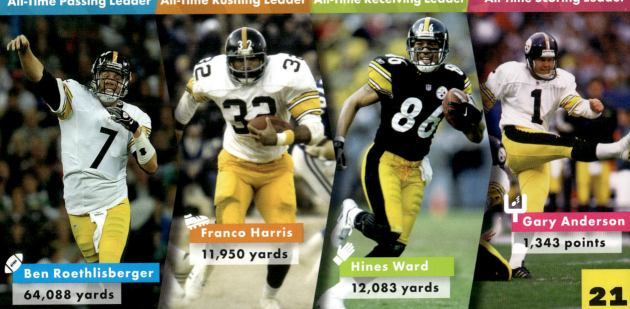

All-Time Passing Leader   All-Time Rushing Leader   All-Time Receiving Leader   All-Time Scoring Leader

Ben Roethlisberger
64,088 yards

Franco Harris
11,950 yards

Hines Ward
12,083 yards

Gary Anderson
1,343 points

21

GLOSSARY

division—a group of NFL teams from the same area that often play against each other; there are eight divisions in the NFL.

drafted—chose a college athlete to play for a professional team

field goal—a score in football worth three points

mascot—an animal or symbol that represents a sports team

playoffs—games played after the regular season is over; playoff games determine which teams play in the championship game.

quarterback—a player whose main job is to throw and hand off the ball

rival—a long-standing opponent

running back—a player whose main job is to run with the ball

stadium—an arena where sports are played

Super Bowls—annual championship games of the NFL

TO LEARN MORE

AT THE LIBRARY

Bailey, Diane. *The Story of the Pittsburgh Steelers*. Minneapolis, Minn.: Kaleidoscope, 2020.

Hill, Christina. *Inside the Pittsburgh Steelers*. Minneapolis, Minn.: Lerner Publications, 2023.

Meier, William. *Pittsburgh Steelers*. Minneapolis, Minn: Abdo Publishing, 2020.

ON THE WEB

FACTSURFER

Factsurfer.com gives you a safe, fun way to find more information.

1. Go to www.factsurfer.com.

2. Enter "Pittsburgh Steelers" into the search box and click $\mathcal{Q}$.

3. Select your book cover to see a list of related content.

INDEX